# School Buses
## on the Go

by Beth Bence Reinke

LERNER PUBLICATIONS ◆ MINNEAPOLIS

**Note to Educators:**

Throughout this book, you'll find critical thinking questions. These can be used to engage young readers in thinking critically about the topic and in using the text and photos to do so.

Lerner Publications Company
A division of Lerner Publishing Group, Inc.
241 First Avenue North
Minneapolis, MN 55401 USA

For reading levels and more information, look up this title at www.lernerbooks.com.

**Library of Congress Cataloging-in-Publication Data**

The Cataloging-in-Publication Data for *Garbage Trucks on the Go* is on file at the Library of Congress.
978-1-5124-8251-5 (lib. bdg.)
978-1-5415-1116-3 (pbk.)
978-1-5124-8260-7 (EB pdf)

Manufactured in the United States of America
1 – CG – 12/31/17

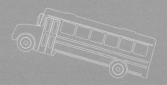

LERNER
e
SOURCE

Expand learning beyond the printed book. Download free, complementary educational resources for this book from our website, www.lerneresource.com.

# Table of Contents

# School Buses

School buses are yellow.

They pick up students.

They take students

to school.

A school bus has six wheels.

Two are at the front.

Four are in the back.

Mirrors help the driver see.

**Why do you think school buses have so many mirrors?**

There is a door at the back.

Kids can go out the back door if there

is an emergency.

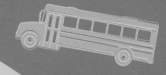

The bus stops.

Signal lights flash.

A stop sign arm pops out.

It tells other drivers to stop.

**Why is it important for other drivers to stop?**

A crossing arm moves out.

It shows kids where to walk.

That way the bus driver can

see them.

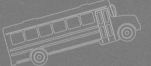

crossing arm

The driver opens the door.

Cars stop and wait while kids get

on the bus.

Students climb the bus stairs.

They hold onto the handrail.

There are seats on each side

of the aisle.

Why should
you use the
handrail while
getting on
the bus?

This bus has a wheelchair lift.

It lifts students onto the bus.

# Picture Glossary

**aisle**
the path between bus seats where students walk

**crossing arm**
a bar that helps students walk far enough in front of the bus

**lift**
a device that lifts wheelchairs into the bus

**signal lights**
red and yellow lights that flash when the bus is stopping

23

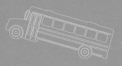

# Read More

Bellisario, Gina. *Be Aware!* Minneapolis: Millbrook Press, 2014.

Garrett, Winston. *Let's Ride the School Bus!* New York: PowerKids Press, 2015.

Jennings, Rosemary. *Safe on the School Bus.* New York: PowerKids Press, 2017.

# Index

## Photo Credits

The images in this book are used with the permission of: © Stuart Monk/Shutterstock.com, pp. 4–5; © eyewave/iStock.com, pp. 6–7; © Ann Baldwin/iStock.com, p. 9; © DouglasFord/iStock.com, pp. 10, 23 (bottom right); © legenda/Shutterstock.com, pp. 12–13, 23 (top right); © lisegagne/iStock.com, p. 15; © kali9/iStock.com, pp. 16, 23 (top left); © Jaren Jai Wicklund/Shutterstock.com, pp. 19, 23 (bottom left); © Thepalmer/iStock.com, p. 20; © Norbert Rehm/Shutterstock.com, p. 22.

Front Cover: © mokee81/iStock.com.